CCB-B
HB Guide BL1994
Ent W
PW

SEP 1999

19253

Center for Children's/Young Adult Books
College of Education
Mankato State University
Mankato, MN 56001

Unless Recalled Earlier

D1265719

The
KING'S
FOOL

A Book
about
Medieval

and
Renaissance
Fools

"If you wish to look at a fool you have not far to go.
You have only to look in a mirror."
—Seneca, Roman philosopher in the first century

Words and pictures by DANA FRADON

DUTTON CHILDREN'S BOOKS • NEW YORK

Copyright © 1993 by Dana Fradon

All rights reserved.

Library of Congress Cataloging-in-Publication Data
Fradon, Dana.
The king's fool: a book about medieval and renaissance fools /
words and pictures by Dana Fradon.—1st ed.
p. cm.
Summary: Examines the role of fools or jesters in medieval and
renaissance society and describes such individuals as Will Sommers
of sixteenth-century England and Querno of sixteenth-century Italy.
ISBN 0-525-45074-2
1. Fools and jesters—Juvenile literature. 2. Renaissance—
Juvenile literature. [1. Fools and jesters.] I. Title.
GT3670.F73   1993
792.7'028'0940902—dc20   92-43836 CIP AC

Published in the United States 1993 by
Dutton Children's Books,
a division of Penguin Books USA Inc.
375 Hudson Street, New York, New York 10014

Designed by Barbara Powderly

Printed in Hong Kong   First edition
10 9 8 7 6 5 4 3 2 1

ERC
Juv.
GT
3670
.F73
1993

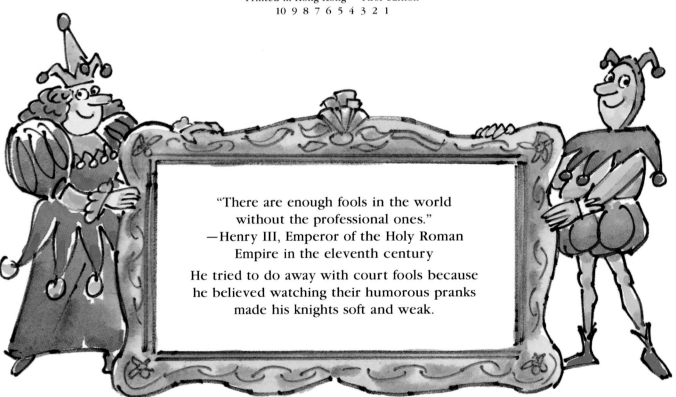

"There are enough fools in the world
without the professional ones."
—Henry III, Emperor of the Holy Roman
Empire in the eleventh century

He tried to do away with court fools because
he believed watching their humorous pranks
made his knights soft and weak.

To my mother
and father

"All young persons would be the better
for being made to wear the fool's emblems
for seven years, and if for one hour of that time
such persons denied themselves to be fools
they should be made to begin the period
all over again."
—Maximilian II, Emperor of the Holy Roman
Empire in the sixteenth century

When you come to a colored dot in the text, find the
same-colored dot below for a little more information.

● ● ● ●

In the medieval room of a great museum, Miss Quincy and her class are looking at some small statues. The statues are of five men and one woman whose job it was to make people laugh. They were the comedians and humorists of ages past. They performed hundreds of years ago. People called them various names: fools, jesters, jokers, and buffoons.

The guard assures them that if you press the right button, anything can happen. TV sets and VCRs go on, lamps light up, rockets lift off.... And Frambert? Press the right button and he becomes almost human.

The students applaud Frambert's acrobatics, and Frambert bows to them.

"Thank you, friends! The guard could not have chosen a better man to tell you about fools. In the past, the strange fraternity of fools included many of the sharpest wit and many who had but half a wit.● Some were rascals and others heroes. Some became rich and others died penniless.

"Imagine! What if each of you had your own private comedian to amuse you, cheer you up, and even give you wise advice? Well, in medieval and renaissance● days, kings, queens, popes, and other powerful, wealthy people had just that. Each had a fool, or many fools, of their very own. We fools were constant companions to our masters or mistresses, almost like pets.

"By being funny, we earned our keep. But we did much more—as you shall see.

● That is, some fools were smart and clever; others were not.
● roughly the period from the ninth century into the seventeenth

"People have always enjoyed laughing, so it wasn't hard for those with comic talent to learn that being a joker could be profitable.

"Even a thousand or more years before I was born, fools of the ancient courts were as sharp-tongued and funny as those of my day. Galba, a fool belonging to the Roman emperor Augustus,● once pretended to be asleep at the dinner table while a guest whispered compliments to the hostess. He was giving them privacy. But, *hah!* When another guest tried to steal extra food from the serving table, which was forbidden, Galba popped awake.

● ruler from 27 BC to AD 14

"Fools came in all shapes and sizes.

"There were male fools and female fools. In medieval days buffoonery was one of the few professions open to women.

"Some fools were thin, almost walking skeletons. Some were so fat they looked like balloons. Just their appearance amused medieval audiences.

"There were giant fools and dwarf fools. Giants were considered impressive, dwarfs cute. Jimmie Camber, who lived in the early 1500s and was the pet dwarf of King James V of Scotland, was said to be 'just over a yard high and two yards in girth.'●

"There were learned fools who specialized in clever wordplay. Some university professors took part-time jobs as buffoons to supplement their meager teaching salaries. Buffoonery paid so well, many gave up teaching entirely.

● two yards around the waist

"Fools fell into two groups, 'artificial' and 'natural.' Artificial fools were usually 'normal'-looking people, with good intelligence, who acted the role of fool. Natural fools were drawn from those medieval society considered to be slow-witted or simpleminded, or were physically deformed in some odd, unusual way.

"Medieval folk were not as sensitive to people with mental and physical disabilities as you are today. They were fascinated and amused by them. Although naturals were singled out, they were usually treated well and even held in some awe because they were thought to be magical and to bring good luck.

"Many so-called natural fools—dwarfs, hunchbacks, and so forth—had brilliant minds and were considered by medieval people really to be artificial fools.

"King Henry III of England had a court jester who was also the country's poet laureate. His name was Master Henry. Master Henry was once described as having the legs of a goat, the thighs of a sparrow, the mouth of a hare, the nose of a dog, and the teeth of a bull. Odd-looking, to be sure!

"In their spare time some dwarf-fools were prominent in other professions. Many were lawyers.

● a poet officially honored by his or her country

"Now I'll introduce my clever, crazy colleagues of comedy.

"I'll start with Bertoldo, a dwarf with carrot red hair and eyebrows as stiff as pig bristles. He lived fifteen hundred years ago in Lombardy, a region in Italy. His career began on a whim. The penniless Bertoldo strolled off the street into a king's court and sat down right next to the monarch. The king's name was Alboin.

● meaningless sounds uttered by fools

"Bertoldo began making faces at the king. He puffed out his cheeks, crossed his eyes, and stuck out his tongue. The king's court all roared with laughter. King Alboin wondered if this impudent little creature might not make a fine fool, so he tested Bertoldo's wit.

"'What is the best wine?' he asked.

"'Any wine paid for by someone else,' replied Bertoldo.

"'What is the swiftest thing on earth?'

"'Our thoughts,' the dwarf answered.

"King Alboin found Bertoldo's answers quite clever and so made Bertoldo one of his fools.

● medieval for *ice*

"Another fool is Will Sommers, favorite jester of King Henry VIII of England. So famous was Will that an entire play was written about him in Shakespeare's time.

"As a youngster, Will hated to study. To force him to read, his schoolmaster would beat him and his mother would feed him but bread and butter. Apparently their harsh treatment succeeded, because Will could recite from memory hundreds of classical stories, poems, and proverbs. He and the king often exchanged riddles.

● Will was allowed to call King Henry by his nickname.

"Some men fought with swords. Will's weapon was words. He matched wit and wisdom with kings, queens, and church officials. He took joy in insulting everybody and feuded with the king's top adviser, Cardinal Wolsey.

"All this he could do because it amused King Henry. Henry once said to him, 'William, your tongue is privileged.' Fools could say things to kings that would be severely punished—even by death—if others said them.

"Throughout his life, Will was a friend to the poor. He constantly used his influence with the king to help them.

"Still, make no mistake, Will's position at court was that of a fool, and he would often curl up on the floor for the night alongside the king's spaniels.

"The dwarf-fool Querno was a poet, musician, and wit. He lived in Naples, Italy, in the 1500s. Querno had an amazing ability to make up rhymes. Pope Leo X, a great patron● of buffoonery, heard about Querno and decided to add him to his collection of buffoons. He summoned Querno to Rome—a great honor for the tiny fool.

"To create a sensation, Querno made his entrance into Rome riding an elephant and wearing, as a joke, a crown of vines, cabbage leaves, and grapes. From atop the huge beast Querno shouted funny Latin verses that he had composed with the pope in an earlier meeting on the outskirts of the city.

● supporter

"So great was Pope Leo's love for his jokers that they were permitted to enter his chambers unannounced anytime they wished. Visiting officials were not so privileged. They usually faced long delays before they could see the pope. It was jested throughout Rome that an official who wanted to see the pope quickly should dress up in fool's motley—a fool's costume.

"In the 1600s Mathurine was the favored fool of three French kings. She once helped capture an attempted assassin of King Henry IV by blocking the doorway of the king's chambers so the villain could not escape.

"She was known as Mathurine the Amazon because she liked to parade through the streets of Paris dressed as an Amazon●—complete with long flowing robes, armor, a shield, and a wooden spear. She looked as out of place in Paris back then as she would now.

"One day, Mathurine was accompanying a fine lady to an audience with the king. Suddenly, the lady turned to her and angrily said

I DON'T LIKE HAVING A FOOL ON MY RIGHT SIDE.

"Quickly switching to the lady's other side, Mathurine replied

H-M-M-M, IT DOESN'T BOTHER ME AT ALL!

● In Greek mythology, Amazons were a tribe of celebrated women warriors who lived in Asia Minor. The Amazons fought and governed, while men performed the household tasks.

"Mathurine was deeply religious, and just as knights dedicated their swords to God, she dedicated her marotte—the fool's wand she carried in her hand—to God.

"She once heard a visitor to the king brag that while traveling in a distant land, he had seen a colewort● so large that five hundred men could stand in its shade. Mathurine piped up, 'And I did once see a caldron so wide three hundred men it took to carry it.'

"The visitor sneered

HUMPH! AND FOR WHAT WOULD A CALDRON THAT LARGE BE USED?

WHY, SIR, TO BOIL YOUR COLEWORT IN!

● a kind of cabbage

"Now we come to Maître Jehan,● a loyal fool. In 1356, when his master, King John II of France, was captured by the English, Maître Jehan voluntarily accompanied the king to prison.

"Maître Jehan's humor was noted for its common sense. One day in Paris, Maître Jehan spied a poor street cleaner sitting on a cookshop's● doorstep, eating a meager dinner of stale bread. The street cleaner hoped that the smell of roasting meat wafting from the cookshop's open door would make his humble bread more tasty.

● *Master John* in French
● restaurant

"The cookshop owner angrily demanded that the street cleaner pay for the smell. The street cleaner refused—

"—and blows were struck! Maître Jehan stepped between them to settle the argument.

"'Of course the street cleaner should pay!' Maître Jehan said.

"'Street cleaner, though the coins in your purse be few, kindly clink them! You shall pay for the *smell* of roasting meat with the *sound* of money.'

"Now, before I tell you about my own life, a word about several fools I particularly admired.

"There was often great love between masters and their fools. Masters considered compliments to their fools compliments to themselves. Masters were protective of their fools; and in return, some fools risked great danger to protect their masters.

"In 1047 a fool named Gollet overheard a group of noblemen plotting to kill his master, Duke William of Normandy, in his sleep. Gollet rushed to the duke's bedroom, just a step ahead of the would-be assassins. He pounded on the door and shouted a warning to the duke—in rhyme!●

WILLIAM, WILLIAM, HEAR MY CRIES,
THY FOES APPROACH, ARISE, ARISE!
AWAKE, WILLIAM, WHY SLEEPEST THOU?
IF SEIZED THOU WILT BE SLAIN, I TROW!●

● William of Normandy lived to become William I, King of England—William the Conqueror.
● medieval for *believe*

"Fools often spoke in rhyme. They discovered early on that people laughed and paid more attention to a joke told in rhyme. Silly, comic rhyming called doggerel or nonsense verse, often composed on the spot, was an important part of many a fool's act.

"When a young seventeenth-century fool named Triboulet was about to be beaten up by a group of pages● who thought he had insulted them, he lashed out at his attackers in rhyme. Sadly, he was severely beaten. Happily, he recovered and in time became one of France's most famous fools.

● young noblemen beginning their studies to become knights

"Fools felt the same emotions we all feel. Here is a love story about a sixteenth-century French fool named Caillete.

"Caillete's father was the chief fool of King Francis I. Caillete was a handsome, intelligent young man—and not yet a fool. While visiting his father at court, Caillete caught the attention of the count de Saint-Vallier. The count was so impressed by Caillete that he took him into his household—a great privilege for a fool's son.

"Caillete became the constant companion of the count's beautiful daughter, Diane. They studied together and played together. Caillete fell in love with her. But Diane was a noblewoman and she married not Caillete, the son of a fool, but the son of a nobleman. Caillete was heartbroken.

"When Caillete's father died, King Francis ordered the nineteen-year-old youth to succeed him as court fool. Caillete reluctantly obeyed. He had wanted to be an army officer.

WHIMPER!

"A few years later the count de Saint-Vallier was accused of treason against King Francis. The fair Diane asked her childhood friend Caillete, who was now Francis's favorite fool, to speak to the king on her father's behalf. Caillete named his price: If the king pardoned her father, Diane must kiss her old fool friend before the entire court of France.

"Caillete succeeded—the king forgave Diane's father. Alas, Caillete grew very ill. Some say he was poisoned, but no one knows why or by whom. His kiss, from the woman of his dreams, came as he was drawing his last breath. Some say he died blissfully, but, well…who knows?

"Now I'd like to tell you about myself. I was born about 1530● in the kingdom of Domania.● I was of humble birth, as were most fools. My parents were hardworking farmers, a little better-off than peasants.

"As a youngster I showed a talent for making people laugh. I could mimic the way people talked, walked, and gestured. I read all the popular jest books.● Speaking in rhyme came easily, and I had a way with animals. Birds, dogs, pigs, ducks, and cats loved to perform with me.

"Word of my abilities reached the king of Domania, and he sent several courtiers to look me over. They invited me to live in the king's castle. With more education and experience they thought I would make a fine fool.

"The king gave my parents a substantial sum of money; they could visit me whenever they wished. If I didn't like my new life I was always free to leave.

● In medieval days, accurate records of humble folks' births were not always kept.
● an imaginary kingdom, as Frambert is an imaginary fool
● books of jokes often written by fools

"At nineteen I officially became one of the king's fools. There was no ceremony; the king simply gave me my costume, my fool's motley. It was expensive. Each piece was designed and sewn by the royal tailor. Masters and mistresses often spent more money on their fool's motley than they did on their children's clothing. A spectacular-looking fool was a sign of importance and wealth.

"My hood was called a coxcomb because it resembled a rooster's red head, but it also sported two donkey's ears with bells at the tips.

"One of my marottes had on the end a soft leather bladder● filled with peas. Other marottes had a fool's head on the end. It was, you might say, the fool's magic wand—wave it and people laughed.

"Whether working, playing, or even sleeping, what I wore always identified me—I say proudly—as a fool.

● the bladder from a pig, cow, or horse

"The king had five fools; I was the newest. As in any career, one starts at the bottom. My first duty was to be the king's cock-crower.

"All night long I signaled the hour by crowing like a rooster. This was for the benefit of the guards, cooks, and bakers, the servants who tended the fires, and any others who might be working on the castle's many chores. At dawn I was joined by the real roosters outside. Together, we awakened the entire castle.

"There were simple clocks in my day, even clocks with hammers that struck bells every hour. Still, the ancient tradition of the cock-crower lived on. I guess it added a touch of human warmth to the long, dark night.

"Our masters and mistresses often followed the advice we jesters gave them. Because we were generally pampered, some of us became arrogant and conceited. I was no different from most, at least when I was young. I felt superior to the castle's servants and most other ordinary folk I met.

"One day I teased a huge butcher named Ragenold. He was a pleasant soul—until aroused by my obnoxious behavior. Ragenold threatened to chop my head off. Maybe he was only fooling, but I was filled with fear and ran to the king for protection.

FEAR NOT, FRAMBERT, HE SHALL NOT CUT OFF THY HEAD. IF HE DOES, I SHALL HANG HIM THE NEXT DAY AFTER.

NAY, I PRAY, SIRE, I WOULD RATHER YOU HUNG HIM A DAY BEFORE!

"At supper we fools sat at a special table below the royal table, entertaining everybody as we ate.

"One evening the king heard one of his guests make a stupid remark. He smiled slyly at me and shouted, 'Frambert, get me a list of all the blockheads in Domania!' I answered, 'Sire, that would take too long. But if you want a list of the wise men, you shall have it in two minutes!' Everybody laughed.

"Not all the amusement we gave that night was based on clever remarks. Our behavior was often silly, even disgusting. The half-wit fools were fed bits of horrible food, like the flesh of crows and monkeys. Today, you know it's rude and unjust to ridicule or laugh at people with disabilities or infirmities—but, alas, at that supper, well…everybody laughed.

"Some fools pranced around, striking guests gently on the head with their marottes in mock attack, or crept up behind them and tickled them.

"One fool attempted to whisk a tablecloth out from under the dishes. With a great flourish he gave it a mighty yank. The sounds of broken glass, clattering crockery, and laughter rang through the dining hall. The fool had failed—as always—but, as always, his audience loved it.

"Sometimes the climax of the evening was a food fight. Food fights were not to my liking. It was a medieval custom to save leftovers for the poor—but… everybody laughed!

THIS IS MY FAVORITE KIND OF HUMOR!

"The tournament, or joust, was medieval Europe's favorite sport. Two knights armed with lances spurred their mounts to a full gallop from opposite ends of the field. The object of this bloody sport was to knock your opponent off his horse, even if it meant injuring or killing him.

"Between jousts some light entertainment was wanted. Often we fools, armed with wooden swords, would stage a mock battle. The crowd found this very funny. Fun it was, though occasionally some of us got hurt.

"Sometimes fools fought for real. In medieval times, battles were not always settled by whole armies. Once in a while, to avoid great bloodshed, the opposing sides would each select a champion—their best warrior—to do battle for them. In 1461 the king of Hungary and the king of Bohemia grew tired of their war. As a lark, each king named his favorite fool to be his champion and promised to abide by the results.

"The fools fought furiously with their wooden swords, fists, and feet. The Bohemian was big, the Hungarian smaller, but the Hungarian won.

"Often the best medicine for a sick person is just to be entertained and cheered up. Once, when my king was ill, his doctors wrote the following prescription: 'Recipe Frambert. Honest mirth,● especially at dinner, supper, and bedtime.' To help him get well, I would ask the king riddles by the hour. He loved them! Who doesn't? Even when I read him his messages I would make humorous comments about the pompous officials who wrote them. My pet monkey, Ermitrude, amused him by opening the letters.

"The fifteenth-century Italian fool Matello was such a success at healing with humor that when he entered a sickroom he was received as if he were a great doctor.

"There was an odd dance craze in my time called the Morris. It is thought to have developed from the jerky, exaggerated movements fools used when poking fun at the way the noble classes danced.

"Morris dancers, each doing his or her own little jig, paraded through the streets of a village. Sometimes they got quite boisterous and were arrested. One group danced from London to Norwich, about one hundred forty miles, in nine days.

"Morris dancers wore costumes representing characters from the Robin Hood legend, adorned with noisy bells. They were always led by a real fool.● I myself led Morris dancers several times.

● An ordinary person impersonating the fool could be arrested.

"I retired from buffoonery when I was about fifty-five years old. My son and daughter both became jesters.

"Many fools lived in poverty after retirement, but favored jesters often received generous pensions. A German fool named Clause Hintze was given an entire village named Buttondorf.● He renamed it Hintzendorf.

"I never dreamed that would happen to me, but it did! The king gave me a tiny village that he named Frambertville. My wife and I governed the village—wisely, I hope. It prospered, and we prospered. I even managed to write several jest books and a successful funny play.

"Oh, yes! The king honored me one more way. He had a sculptor carve a small statue of me and displayed it at court.

● Button village

"I retired just before court buffoonery came to an end. The parliamentary governments of the 1600s were less-willing targets of a fool's wit than the monarchies of the past had been. Also, as average citizens gained more freedom, they often said things about their society that before only fools would have had the privilege to say. People read more; it was cheaper to buy jest books than to keep a fool. People also went to the theater more often.

"To survive, displaced court fools began performing in taverns, carnivals, and fairs, and on the streets. Some were thrown in jail. The strict new governments often judged their jokes to be vulgar or obscene and, therefore, a bad influence on the common people. Still other fools were imprisoned simply for poking fun at their government as they once poked fun at their king.

● a more representative government than were monarchies

"The wisest words in medieval and early renaissance plays were always spoken by the actors who played fools. But by the late 1600s, the character of fool had almost disappeared from the stage.

"In 1662 a fool stepped onto the stage before each performance of *Thorney Abbey,* a play about a king, and protested the lack of a fool in the production.

"He said

"Soon, professional funny people were no longer referred to as fools, jesters, or buffoons. They were called merry-andrews and jack-puddings in England; jean pottages in France; zanies and macaronis in Italy. Eventually, they would simply be called—as they are today—comedians, comics, or clowns.

"Probably the last household fool in England was Dicky Pearce, a natural fool belonging to the earl of Suffolk. Dicky died in 1728. On his tombstone there is a poem by Jonathan Swift:

"Here lies the Earl of Suffolk's fool,
Men called him Dicky Pearce;
His folly helped to make folks laugh,
When wit and mirth were scarce.

"Poor Dick, alas! is dead and gone;
What good is it to cry?
Dickies enough are left behind
To laugh at by and by."

That is the end of Frambert's lecture. But as he and the guard wave good-bye to the students, Frambert can't resist one last riddle:

Cantor Jr. Library/Young Adult Books

Curriculum ~~~~ ~~~~ tion
Mankato State University
Mankato, MN 56001